AND ALL GOD'S CHILDREN
SAID AMEN

Praying the Scriptures for Every Season of a Child's Life

Pamela Govender

 A catalogue record for this book is available from the National Library of Australia

Copyright © 2025 Pamela Govender

All rights reserved.

ISBN-13: 978-1-923174-75-7

Linellen Press
265 Boomerang Road
Oldbury, Western Australia
helen.iles.linpress@gmail.com

Table of Contents

Introduction 6

The Lord's Prayer 8

Prayer for our dads, granddads, and uncles 12

Prayer for our mums, grandmas, and aunts 16

A Prayer for Forgiveness 20

Prayer for Courage 25

Prayer for Healing 31

Prayer for Gratitude 37

Prayer for Peaceful Sleep 42

Prayer for Myself 47

A Prayer for Salvation 52

About the Author 58

Introduction

Two very close friends, Leelee the Lion and Lala the Lamb, live in a beautiful place called Rainbow River. The river sparkles with many pretty colours when the sun shines on it, making it look like a real rainbow.

Leelee and Lala love their home. It's where they go on many adventures and create many happy memories. They are best friends, and their special friendship brings joy to everyone around them.

Leelee, the lion, has a beautiful golden mane. He is known for his strength and courage, and the other animals respect and admire him. But inside, behind his strong appearance, Leelee has a very kind and caring heart.

Lala, on the other hand, is a gentle and graceful lamb. She is shy and always wears a cheerful smile. Lala is known for her ability to bring joy and peace to all those around her.

The Lord's Prayer

Leelee and Lala loved attending Sunday school. Every Sunday, they happily joined their friends to learn about faith, kindness, and the teachings of Jesus.

Their Sunday school teacher, Mam Pam, began by saying, "Today, we're going to talk about something very special — the Lord's Prayer.

Although Leelee and Lala had heard of this prayer before, they were not quite sure what it meant.

Mam Pam, with a warm smile, said, "The Lord's Prayer is like a beautiful gift from God to us. It helps us talk to God and tell him what is in our hearts, like our thoughts, hopes and feelings. It's like having a caring talk with God, our Heavenly Father. The Lord's Prayer helps us remember important things Jesus taught, like being kind, saying thank you, and asking God to help us make good choices.

When we say this prayer, we're inviting God into our hearts and asking for His love and wisdom.

"Today, we are going to learn The Lord's Prayer. It's like special words we can use when we need comfort, strength, and help in our lives. It's a reminder that God is always with you, listening and caring for you."

As Leelee and Lala repeated the prayer with their friends, it made them feel happy and close to each other. They realised that learning the Lord's Prayer was not just a lesson in Sunday school, but a special treasure they could keep with them as they grow in their faith.

Can you say the Lord's Prayer?

The Lord's Prayer is found in the Bible in Matthew 6:9-13.

This is where Jesus teaches his disciples how to pray.

Let's Pray

Our Father who art in heaven,

hallowed be thy name.

Thy kingdom come.

Thy will be done

on earth as it is in heaven.

Give us this day our daily bread,

and forgive us our trespasses,

as we forgive those who trespass against us,

and lead us not into temptation,

but deliver us from evil.

For thine is the kingdom and the power, and the glory,

forever and ever.

Amen.

Prayer for our dads, granddads, and uncles

Today is a very special day in Rainbow River. It is Father's Day – a day to celebrate all the fathers, granddads, and uncles who fill their lives with love and laughter. The friends know they are surrounded by very nice people who care for them and teach them important life lessons.

Leelee and Lala have fun memories of camping with their dads, granddads, and uncles. They remember sitting by the campfire, toasting marshmallows, and telling stories while gazing at the sky's shiny stars. They also remember cool adventures, like walking in the woods, fishing in the lake, and exploring Rainbow River. It was so much fun!

With hearts full of gratitude and love, Leelee and Lala decide it is time to say a special prayer to thank God for the dads, granddads, and uncles in their lives.

Can you say a prayer for all the special dads, granddads, and uncles in your life?

Let's Pray

Dear Lord Jesus,

I come to you today with a thankful heart for all the special dads, granddads, and uncles in my life. Help them, dear Lord, to live in a way that makes you happy. Guide their thoughts and actions and may they shine like a bright light wherever they go.

Lord, I ask you to give all fathers peace and courage. Protect them from saying or doing things that might hurt others. Keep them safe and healthy as they care for their families.

We ask all these things in the mighty name of Jesus.

Amen.

Now let's learn this Bible verse.

Ephesians 6:2

Honour your father and mother, which is the first commandment with a promise, so that it may go well with you and that you may enjoy long life on the earth.

Prayer for our mums, grandmas, and aunts

Mother's Day is just around the corner, and Leelee and Lala are so excited. They want to do something extra special for their mums, grandmas and aunts. These amazing women have always been their biggest supporters and have always watched over them with so much love and care. They want to celebrate them, as they fill their lives with love and warmth.

They deserve some pampering, so the friends decide to make personalised vouchers for them.

They make vouchers promising a nail painting session, a relaxing shoulder massage, and foot massages.

On Mother's Day, they present the gift vouchers with big smiles. The mums, aunts and grandmas are touched by the thoughtful and heartfelt gifts.

It is a beautiful way to show their love and appreciation, making Mother's Day so special.

With hearts full of gratitude and love, Leelee and Lala decide it is time to say a special prayer to thank God for the mums, grandmas, and aunts in their lives.

Can you say a prayer for all the special mums, grandmas and aunts in your life?

Let's Pray

Dear Lord Jesus,

Thank you for our mums, grandmas and aunts in our lives.

I thank you, Lord, for their love, care and sacrifice. Lord, I pray that they will always look to you, and they may never be afraid. Lord, I ask that you give our mothers peace, joy, love and happiness. May you always bless them. Give our mothers the strength to care for families and always guide their children.

Watch over them, protect them, and fill their hearts with peace and love.

In Jesus' name, I pray

Amen.

Now let's learn this Bible verse.

Ephesians 6:1

    Children, obey your parents in the Lord, for this is right.

A Prayer for Forgiveness

Leelee and Lala, the two best friends, love going on fun adventures together, like exploring the forest, finding hidden treasures, and playing with their favourite colourful ball.

One day while playing, Leelee got so excited he kicked the ball way too hard, hurting Lala's nose. Ouch! screamed Lala in pain, as tears filled her eyes.

Leelee felt really bad and rushed to help his dear friend. "I am so sorry, Lala. I didn't mean to hurt you."

As Lala wiped away her tears, she said, "I know it was just an accident, Leelee."

Leelee felt sad and said, "I wish I hadn't kicked it so hard. I should have been more careful."

Lala gave a gentle smile and said, "Leelee, friends forgive each other when accidents happen. I forgive you."

Leelee felt happy again and gave Lala a big hug.

From that day on, Leelee and Lala continued to play, laugh, and have fun adventures in Rainbow River. They knew that forgiveness in friendship is like a special gift you give to your friend when they make a mistake or hurt your feelings. It's like saying, "I understand that you didn't mean to do something wrong, and I'm not going to be mad at you anymore." When you forgive your friend, it helps heal any hurt feelings and makes your friendship stronger."

Leelee and Lala taught us something very important about forgiveness through their friendship. We saw how forgiveness made their bond even stronger. In the Bible, we learned from the story of the Prodigal Son that forgiveness is a wonderful and powerful thing. In that story, a son makes some big mistakes but is still forgiven and loved by his father when he comes back. This teaches us that forgiveness can mend hearts and bring people closer together. So, the story of the Prodigal Son and Leelee and Lala teaches us that forgiveness is a special gift we can give to the people we care about.

Can you ask mum or dad to tell you the story of the Prodigal Son, so you can learn more about forgiveness?

Let's Pray

Our dear heavenly father, I come before you today with a grateful heart for your love and understanding. Thank you for the gift of forgiveness. Lord, I know that sometimes, people do things that hurt me, and it's not always easy to forgive them. But I know you forgive me when I make mistakes, so I want to be able to forgive others too.

Please help me let go of any anger or sadness in my heart. Teach me love and care for others.

Thank you for your patience and for showing me the way of forgiveness. I want to grow up to be a person who forgives and loves others just as you do.

In Jesus' name, I pray,

Amen.

Now let's learn this Bible verse.

Ephesians 4:32

Be kind and compassionate to one another, forgiving each other, just as in Christ God forgave you.

Prayer for Courage

Leelee and Lala shared many adventures together, but one day, they faced a challenge that showed just how brave they were.

There was a big, scary storm in Rainbow River. The sky turned dark, lightning flashed, and thunder roared. All the animals in Rainbow River gathered close because they were very scared of the powerful storm.

Leelee and Lala watched as the other animals looked for shelter. They could have hidden away too, but they knew they needed to help their friends in need.

The rain poured and the wind howled as Leelee and Lala went out into the storm. They knew there was a family of rabbits that lived in a burrow near the riverbank. As the water rose, it started sloshing into their burrow, and their home was in danger of flooding.

As Leelee and Lala got closer, they saw that the rabbit's burrow was almost underwater. The rabbits were all huddled together, looking scared and cold.

Leelee and Lala knew they needed to help right away.

They had an idea. Leelee, who was strong, used rocks and logs to make a wall to keep the water away from the rabbit's home. He worked hard, moving heavy things to keep the water out.

At the same time, Lala, who was very kind, took care of the scared baby rabbits. She talked to them softly, telling them that everything would be okay. She made sure they felt safe, even when it was all a bit scary.

As the water kept going up, Leelee and Lala's teamwork really helped. The wall they made stayed strong, and the water went away from the rabbit's house. The rabbits were safe and dry because of Leelee's and Lala's bravery. The animals of Rainbow River cheered their brave friends.

Here we see that Leelee and Lala had protected the rabbits, just as David in the Bible protected his people from Goliath.

You see, a long time ago, there was a giant named Goliath who scared everyone. But a young boy named David, who was small but very brave, faced Goliath with just a sling and a stone. David's courage and faith helped him defeat the giant, just as Leelee and Lala's bravery had protected the rabbits.

Can you ask Mum or Dad to tell you the story of David and Goliath, so you can learn more about courage and faith?

Let's Pray

Dear Lord Jesus, I thank you for all that you have done for me. Even when things get difficult, help me remember that you are with me. Please give me courage and faith when I am feeling scared or unsure, and help me know that you will not leave me.

Lord, help me see you, hear you, and trust you. Help me to believe in myself, just like you do. Father, I know you made me strong, loving, and smart, not scared.

Bless me with the same courage you gave to David as he fought the giant Goliath, because he knew that you were in control.

Lord, with your love, I feel brave, and I know that you are watching over me. Thank you for being my friend and guiding me. I love you, Lord.

Amen.

Now let's learn this Bible verse.

Joshua 1:9

Have I not commanded you? Be strong and courageous. Do not be afraid; do not be discouraged, for the Lord your God will be with you wherever you go.

Prayer for Healing

Today, Leelee and Lala are very excited to go to school. They love going to school every day. They enjoy making new friends and seeing their favourite teacher, Miss Annie. She is kind, patient, and always has a big smile.

As they enter their classroom, they notice that their teacher, Miss Annie, is not at her desk.

With a worried look, Leelee asks, "Where is Miss Annie today, Lala?"

Lala looks around; her gentle eyes also fill with concern. "I don't know, Leelee.

Just then, Mr Rods, the school principal, enters the room. "Good morning, students," he says. "I have some sad news to share. Miss Annie is not feeling well, and she's in the hospital to get better."

Leelee and Lala like Miss Annie very much and are very worried about her.

Mr Rods continues. "We need to help Miss Annie feel better. Let's create get-well cards to show her how much we care and hope she gets better soon."

The classroom fills with activity as the students work on their colourful cards. They draw pictures of smiling suns, rainbows, and flowers to bring cheer to Miss Annie.

After finishing their cards, the class gathers around Mr Rods and place their cards in a big envelope.

"We will send these cards to Miss Annie, and I am sure they will make her feel much better," Mr Rods says with a warm smile. "Can we also say a special prayer of healing for Miss Annie?"

They hold hands and pray for their dear teacher. They begin to speak to Jesus, knowing he can perform miracles.

Leelee and Lala beam with pride, knowing that their prayer and kindness have played a part in Miss Annie's recovery. They understand that, just like the story of Jesus healing the paralysed man with the help of his friends who lowered him through the roof, they too have shown the power of love and friendship in helping someone in need.

Can you ask Mum or Dad to tell you the story of how Jesus healed the paralysed man, so you can learn more about faith, friendship, and healing.

We too can pray for ourselves when we are feeling sick. Today, let's learn how to say a prayer for healing.

Let's Pray

Dear Lord Jesus, I come to you today with a prayer for healing. Please help me feel better, be strong, and be healthy again. Touch me, Lord, with your healing love and make me feel your comfort. Give the doctors and nurses the wisdom to help me get well soon.

Lord, your word says, by your stripes I am healed, and today I claim this healing over me. Touch me from the crown of my head to the soles of my feet. Strengthen me, guide me, and protect me. Take your rightful place, Lord, and speak life back into my body. Cover me with your precious blood. I pray for victory over this sickness. I know you can do amazing things, and I believe in your love and power. Please watch over me and bring me back to good health.

I ask all this in Jesus' Name,

Amen.

Now let's learn this Bible verse.

Matthew 21:22

If you believe, you will receive whatever you ask for in prayer.

Prayer for Gratitude

It was a cold, rainy day in Rainbow River. Leelee and Lala found themselves unable to go outside for their adventures. So, they decided to play a game indoors in front of the warm, cozy fireplace.

Leelee suggested, "How about we play a game called 'Count My Blessings'? We can take turns sharing all the things we're grateful for. It'll remind us of how much we have to appreciate even on a cold, rainy day."

"That sounds like a wonderful idea, Leelee. You can start!" said Lala.

Leelee began, "I'm grateful for a warm home that keeps us dry, even when it's raining outside.

Lala smiled, "I'm thankful for our favourite books, our toys, our board games, our TV, and not forgetting, our warm beds."

Leelee continued, "I'm thankful for our friendship, Lala. You are my best friend, and I love our adventures together."

Lala's eyes lit up as she replied, "Leelee, I'm grateful for our families. Imagine being all alone."

Leelee nodded, "And I'm thankful for all the delicious food we have."

As they continued taking turns, the friends had so much to be grateful and thankful for.

By the end of their game, the rain had stopped. Lala looked at Leelee and said, "Leelee, playing 'Count My Blessings' made me realise that we have so much to be thankful for."

Leelee nodded and gave Lala a warm hug. "You're right, Lala. I am even just grateful for being alive. Gratitude makes us appreciate all that we have and find happiness in the present moment.

Gratitude is not just about saying 'thank you' but about truly feeling thankful in your heart.

What are you grateful for today? Why don't you play that game, Count My Blessings and list all that you are thankful for.

Let's Pray

Dear Lord Jesus, today I come before you with a grateful and thankful heart. Thank you for all that you have given me. As I count my many blessings, big and small, I thank you for it all. Thank you for waking me up this morning. Thank you for all the love, grace, and mercy that you have given me. I thank you for my family, friends, neighbours, and my teachers. I thank you, Lord, for my home and for the food on our table.

I am thankful for the sun, moon, stars, the trees and flowers and the seas. Thank you, Lord, for all the good things in my life. I am grateful for your blessings. Thank you for loving me.

In Jesus' name I pray

Amen.

Now let's learn this Bible verse.

1 Thessalonians 5:18

Rejoice always, pray continually, give thanks in all circumstances; for this is God's will for you in Christ Jesus.

Prayer for Peaceful Sleep

Leelee the Lion was always known for his energy and adventurous spirit.

As mum tucked Leelee into his cozy bed, he would tell her about the excitement of his day and all his adventures. One night, no matter how hard he tried to sleep, he could not. His mind was too busy. He stayed wide awake.

Leelee sat on his bed and talked to God. He asked God for help to stop thinking about what happened during the day, so he could sleep peacefully.

While Leelee prayed, he felt peaceful. He thought about what his mum had told him, that even when you can't sleep, you can find peace by giving your cares and worries to God and trusting in his help.

He lay down, closed his eyes, and let go of his busy thoughts and trusted God to help him. Little by little, he felt his mind calming down, and he felt very relaxed.

He soon fell asleep.

Leelee now knows that even on nights when he cannot sleep, talking to God and trusting in him will bring peace. The next day, he felt very refreshed and excited for more adventures in Rainbow River.

Leelee continued to pray each night, thanking God for the day and asking for peaceful sleep. Over time, he found that these moments of prayer brought comfort and peace to him. He shared this practice with Lala and all their friends. Soon, everyone said a bedtime prayer, trusting that God was watching over them, granting them a peaceful night's sleep.

Can you say a bedtime prayer for a peaceful night's sleep?

Let's Pray

Dear Lord, Today I ask you to calm my heart and my restless mind. I give you all my worries and cares. Bless me now as I rest, Lord. Give me a peaceful night's sleep. I ask for your Angels to watch over me, cover me with your mighty blood and protect me.

Grant me a good night's sleep tonight, so that I can wake up refreshed and ready to begin another day loving you. Help me to fix my eyes and my heart on you. I know, Lord, that, as I sleep now, you will watch over me. Please help me calm my mind and keep away any scary thoughts. I know that fear and worry are not from you. Help me find peace in you. I ask all this in your perfect love.

In the mighty name of Jesus

Amen

Now let's learn this Bible verse.

Matthew 11:28

Come to me, all you who are weary and burdened, and I will give you rest.

Prayer for Myself

Leelee and Lala have always done everything together, but this time, Leelee had to go away with his family for a few days. Lala felt lonely and scared because she had to do a Show and Tell in her class all by herself. She missed the support and encouragement of her best friend.

Lala knew that Leelee couldn't be there, but she remembered the advice he had given her in the past. Leelee always encouraged her to pray when she was scared or worried about anything.

So, on the evening before her Show and Tell, Lala decided to pray. She closed her eyes and began to pray, and trusted God to be there with her and help her.

As she finished her prayer, Lala felt peaceful and happy. She understood that her friend, Leelee, could not always be there, but she knew that she had a friend in Jesus who would always be there and would never leave her.

The next day, Lala stood bravely in front of her class doing her Show and Tell.

As she finished, her classmates clapped loudly, and her teacher was so proud of her for doing such a good job. Lala felt so happy. She knew that God was with her and that prayer had helped her.

She knew that, with prayer, she could always face any challenge and fear, even when her best friend couldn't be by her side.

Lala learned that she should pray for herself, too, not just for others. So, she started praying for herself every day.

Let's Pray

Dear Lord, today I come before you. I thank you, Lord, that I could get up this morning. Please help me to be a nice person and kind to others.

Help me to always be grateful for all that I have. Lord, I cannot do anything without you. I ask for your love, guidance, and for you to always protect me.

Thank you, Lord, for loving me. Thank you that when I am weak, you are strong.

Thank you, Lord, for making me special. Today, I give you all my problems. Forgive me if I have hurt anyone.

Please make my heart gentle and help me speak to everyone with respect. The Bible says you want good things for me. I ask for this blessing in Jesus' name.

Thank you for saving me. I believe you're God's Son who died for my sins and came back to life. Thank you for taking away my sins and giving me eternal life. Come into my heart and be my Saviour.

Amen."

Now let's learn this Bible verse.

Romans 8:28

And we know that in all things God works for the good of those who love him, who have been called according to his purpose.

A Prayer for Salvation

One bright Sunday morning, Leelee and Lala excitedly headed to their Sunday school class.

They were greeted by Mam Pam. "Good morning, children. Today, we're going to talk about something very special called 'Salvation.' Have any of you heard about it before?"

"I am not sure what that means," said Lala.

"That's totally okay," Mam Pam reassured her. "Salvation is wonderful and important. It means being saved by God's love and forgiveness.

Leelee, always eager to learn, asked, "Why do we need to be saved, Mam Pam?"

"We all make mistakes and sometimes do things that aren't very nice," said Mam Pam. "Salvation is like telling God we're sorry when we make mistakes and letting his love show us the right way. It's like getting a fresh start and a chance to be our very best."

"So, how do we get salvation?" Lala asked again.

Mam Pam smiled warmly and replied, "Imagine salvation is like opening the door of your heart to Jesus. You say, 'Please come in, be my friend, and help me do good things.' It's sort of like asking someone to be your best friend forever."

Leelee raised his paw and asked, "Mam Pam, can we pray for salvation?"

"Of course, Leelee," said Mam Pam. "That's a great idea. Let's all pray together."

Let's Pray

Dear Lord Jesus,

I want to learn about your love and follow you all the days of my life. Please come into my heart, show me the way, and forgive me when I do wrong. I want to say with my mouth, and I believe deep in my heart that Jesus is my Lord and Saviour. Thank you for giving me your gift of Salvation, and I am ready to trust you.

Thank you, Lord Jesus, for saving me. Thank you for dying on the cross for me. Lead me on the right path. Thank you for sending your son, Jesus. Thank you for the gift of eternal life. Please, Lord, help me do what you want and become even closer to you every day. Help me become the person you want me to be.

Come into my heart, Lord, and be my Saviour. I give my life to you.

In Jesus' name, I pray.

Amen.

As Leelee and Lala finished saying the prayer, they felt a sense of happiness and joy that comes with accepting salvation. They were so grateful for this opportunity to accept Jesus and for the love and grace they know they have received.

Would you like to pray for Salvation?

How do you feel after saying the Salvation prayer?

Now let's learn this Bible verse.

Romans 10:9

If you declare with your mouth, 'Jesus is Lord,' and believe in your heart that God raised him from the dead, you will be saved.

About the Author

Pamela Govender blends a deep passion for prayer with a heartfelt love for children. A former Sunday School teacher, she is devoted to nurturing faith and planting seeds of Scripture in young hearts. Pamela is a loving wife and proud mother of two wonderful sons.

She is the author of two inspiring books: *Let's Pray About It* and *I Smiled Today*, a comforting guide for those navigating grief and mourning. Through her writing, Pamela encourages parents to make prayer a priority and build a spiritual foundation that will guide their children through every season of life. Her message is clear and timeless:

Train up a child in the way he should go, and when he is old, he will not depart from it." — Proverbs 22:6 (KJV)

www.ingramcontent.com/pod-product-compliance
Lightning Source LLC
Chambersburg PA
CBHW041217240426
43661CB00012B/1073